Ocean Secrets

A Guidebook for Little Underwater Adventurers

words & art by
Sarah Grindler

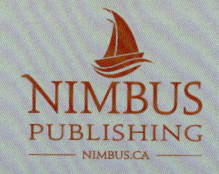

little explorers

NIMBUS PUBLISHING
NIMBUS.CA

Copyright © 2025, Sarah Grindler

All rights reserved. No part of this book may be reproduced, stored in a retrieval system or transmitted in any form or by any means without the prior written permission from the publisher, or, in the case of photocopying or other reprographic copying, permission from Access Copyright, 1 Yonge Street, Suite 1900, Toronto, Ontario M5E 1E5.

Nimbus Publishing Limited
3660 Strawberry Hill Street, Halifax, NS, B3K 5A9
(902) 455-4286 nimbus.ca

Nimbus Publishing is based in Kjipuktuk, Mi'kma'ki, the traditional territory of the Mi'kmaq People.

No part of this book may be used in the training of generative artificial intelligence technologies or systems.

Printed and bound in China
NB1755

Design: Jenn Embree; Editor: Claire Bennet

Library and Archives Canada Cataloguing in Publication

Title: Ocean secrets : a guidebook for little underwater adventurers / words & art by Sarah Grindler.
Names: Grindler, Sarah, author, illustrator.
Description: Series statement: Little explorers
Identifiers: Canadiana (print) 20240507983 | Canadiana (ebook) 20240511565
ISBN 9781774713600 (hardcover) | ISBN 9781774713655 (EPUB)
Subjects: LCSH: Ocean—Juvenile literature. | LCSH: Marine animals—Juvenile literature.
| LCSH: Marine plants—Juvenile literature.
Classification: LCC GC21.5 .G75 2025 | DDC j551.46—dc23

Nimbus Publishing acknowledges the financial support for its publishing activities from the Government of Canada, the Canada Council for the Arts, and from the Province of Nova Scotia. We are pleased to work in partnership with the Province of Nova Scotia to develop and promote our creative industries for the benefit of all Nova Scotians.

To Captain Mike, Voni, and the Octopus

What do you see when you look at the ocean? This gigantic body of salt water covers nearly three quarters of our planet, but so much of it is still a mystery.

We can discover fascinating creatures and incredible plant life by exploring the world's vast and deep seas.

Did you know that an octopus has three hearts?
Or that a crab can regrow a missing claw?

Let's explore some of the secrets of the ocean and the amazing sea life that calls it home. Bring along your water shoes, sunhat, and life jacket, and let's explore.

Before we dip our toes into the cool, salty water, let's explore the shoreline at low tide.

The tide is a name for the way the ocean's water level rises and falls throughout a twenty-four-hour cycle.

The area where the rocky shore and seabed become exposed when the tide is out is called the intertidal zone.

low tide

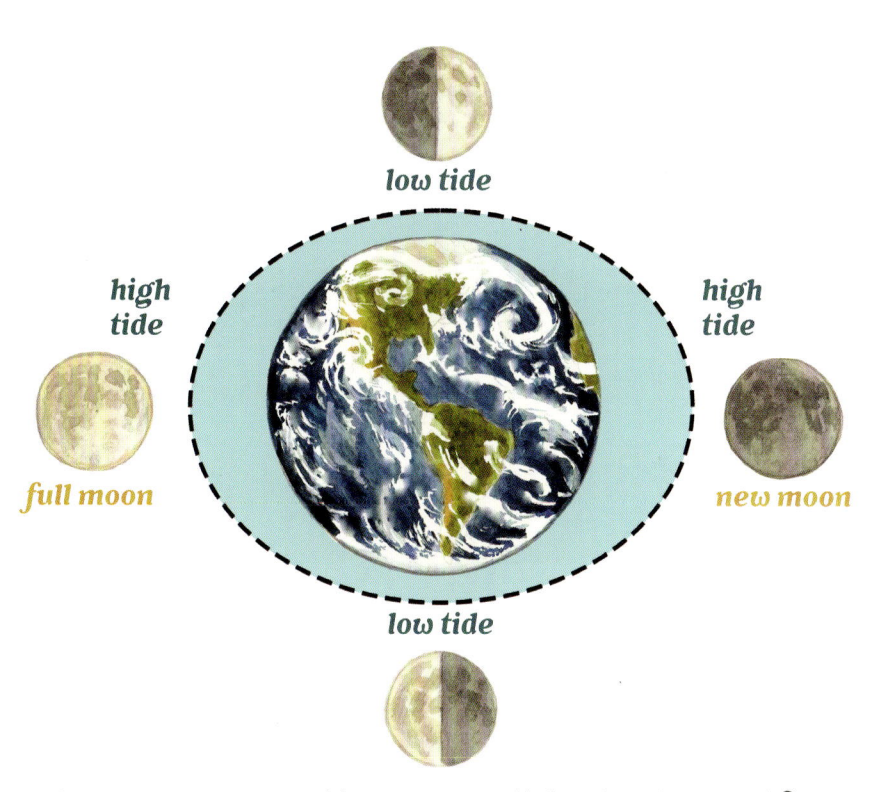

high tide

high tide

full moon

new moon

low tide

The moon causes the ocean's tides to rise and fall using its gravitational pull. On full moons (when the moon is fully visible) and new moons (when the moon is not visible), the sun, earth, and moon are in-line, and this creates the highest and lowest tides. These are called king tides.

periwinkle

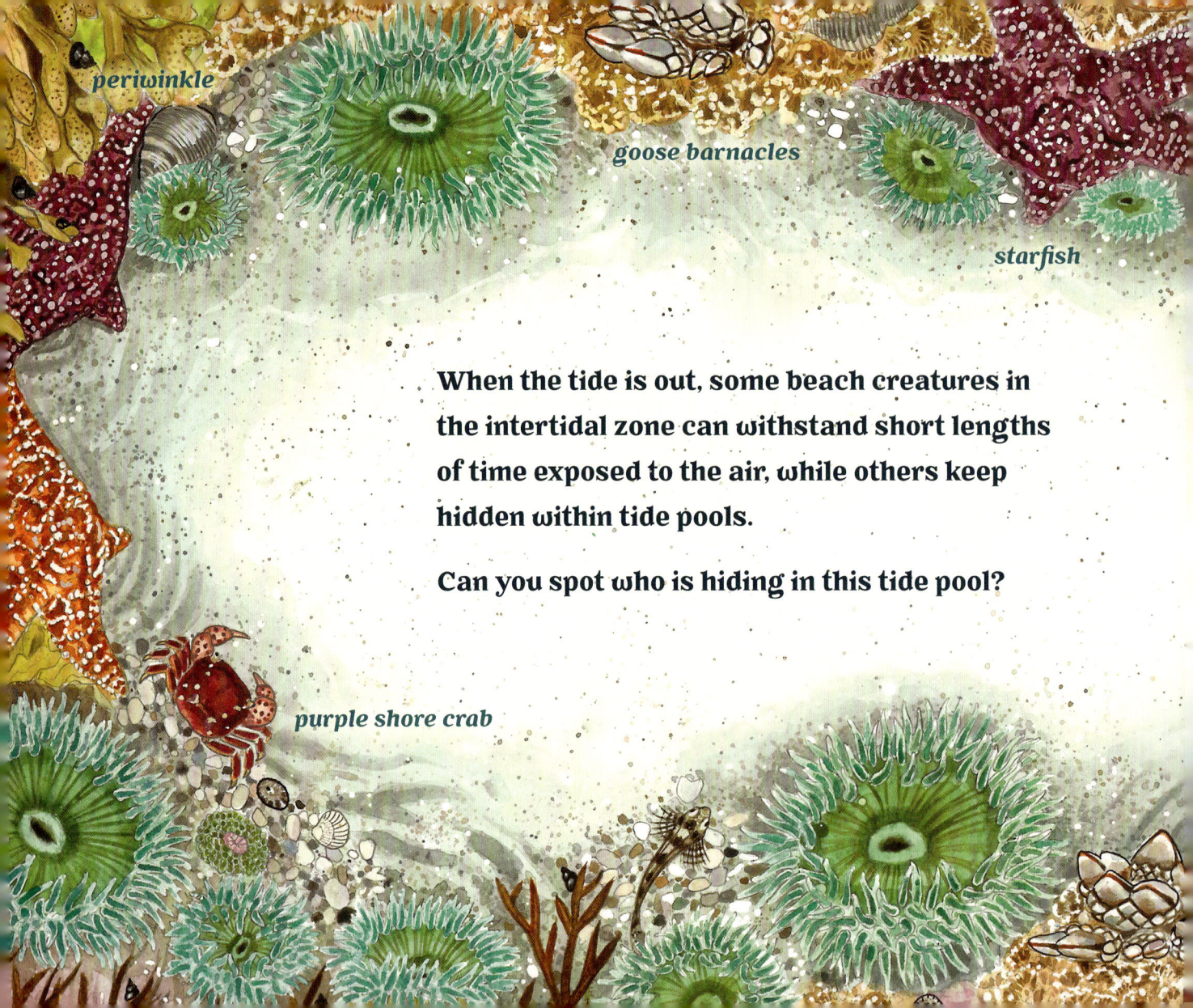

goose barnacles

starfish

When the tide is out, some beach creatures in the intertidal zone can withstand short lengths of time exposed to the air, while others keep hidden within tide pools.

Can you spot who is hiding in this tide pool?

purple shore crab

sculpin

sea urchin   *anemone*   *sea slug*   *hermit crab*

The ocean's zones are determined by how much sunlight reaches the ocean floor.

Many animals and plants need sunlight to thrive, while others prefer to live in deep dark trenches. But most creatures, no matter how far down they live, travel up to the ocean's surface at night for a midnight snack.

This is known as the largest migration on earth.

sunlight zone
200m

twilight zone
1,000m

midnight zone
4,000m

abyssal zone
6,000m

The sunlight zone holds amazing habitats that create safe havens for many creatures.

Kelp forests, made up of brown algae, create safe nurseries for baby sea otters. Their mothers wrap them in the kelp on the surface, then dive below to find food.

Kelp can grow up to 18 inches a day!

Baby fish use seagrass meadows for protection. Urchins and snails enjoy munching on the algae that grow there, and many seabirds and even hammerhead sharks eat the seagrass itself.

Colourful coral reefs are home to thousands, if not millions, of sea creatures. The coral polyps that make up the reefs are actually sac-like animals, not plants. Coral reefs grow as the polyps die off and harden, then more grow on top.

bluefin tuna

Atlantic salmon

sunfish

There are over twenty thousand species of fish in the ocean!

Many are keystone species, meaning they are a crucial part of the food chain.

Atlantic cod

red snapper

clown fish

yellow tang

pufferfish

lionfish

frogfish

canary rockfish

parrotfish

One major keystone species is the salmon.

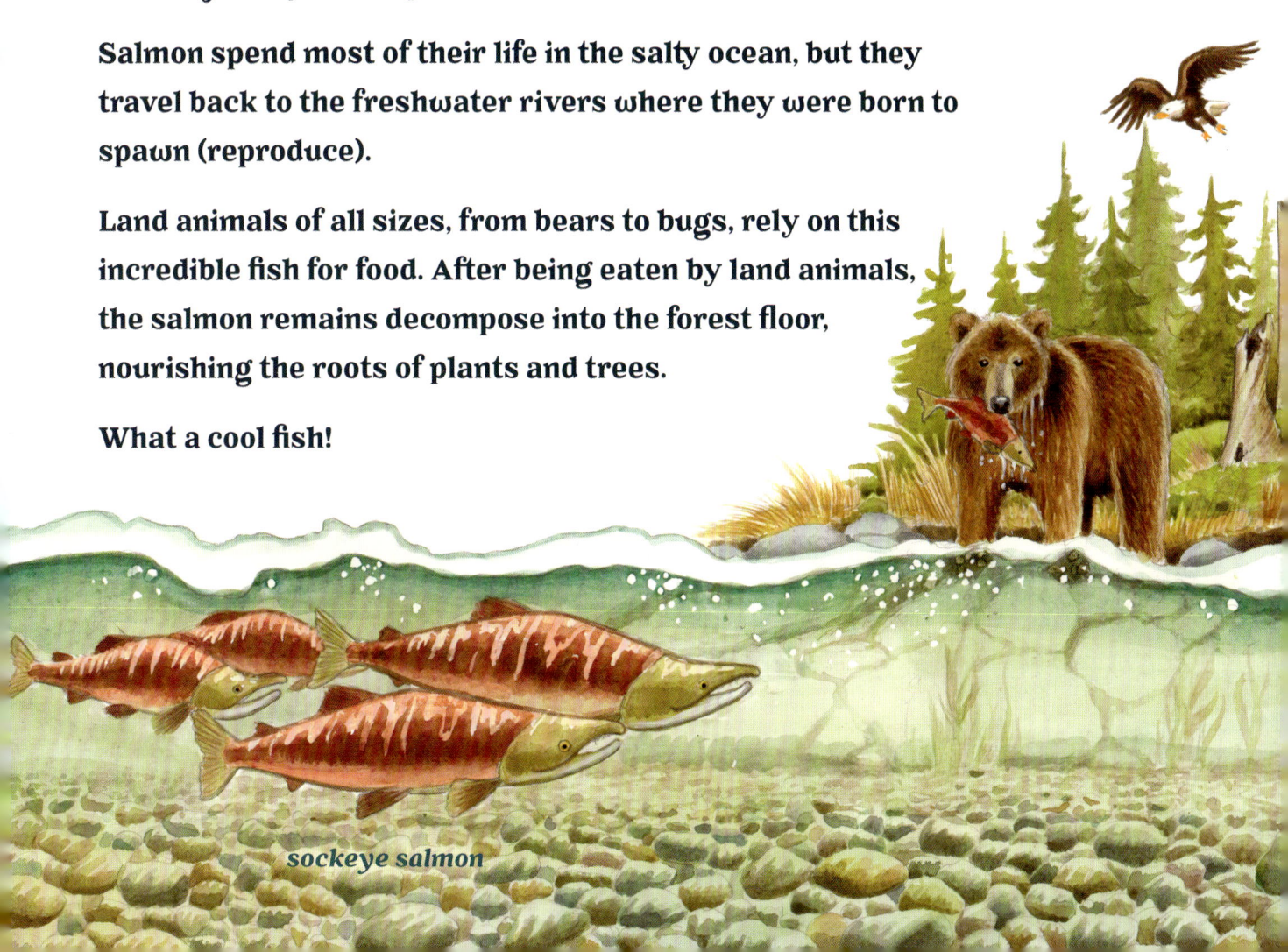

Salmon spend most of their life in the salty ocean, but they travel back to the freshwater rivers where they were born to spawn (reproduce).

Land animals of all sizes, from bears to bugs, rely on this incredible fish for food. After being eaten by land animals, the salmon remains decompose into the forest floor, nourishing the roots of plants and trees.

What a cool fish!

sockeye salmon

Many ocean creatures in the sunlight zone rely on microscopic plankton for their breakfast, lunch, and dinner. ZOOplankton are baby animals, and PHYTOplankton are baby plants.

Where plankton are found, so are krill (tiny crustaceans) and fish. The small fish attract bigger fish into the area, and the bigger fish attract the seals and dolphins, and so on. Even some of the largest creatures of the sea, like the massive whale shark and blue whale, are filter feeders. This means they rely on plankton and krill as their main food source.

plankton

basking shark

plankton close up

humpback whale

North Atlantic right whale

blue whale

Filter-feeding whales are called baleen whales. Humpback whales, right whales, and blue whales are all baleen whales. A full-grown blue whale can eat up to 16 tons of krill per day. Blue whales are the largest animals on the planet. They can weigh up to 180 tons, which is about the same as thirty-six elephants!

Whales, dolphins, and porpoises all live in families called pods and they communicate through clicks and songs. This is called echolocation. Humpback whales all over the world know the same songs!

There are so many amazing species of sharks, including the great white shark. Great whites have an incredible sense of smell.

great white shark

Greenland shark

The deep-dwelling Greenland shark can live for up to five hundred years.

epaulette shark

The epaulette shark can crawl across exposed reefs on their fins.

whale shark

Each whale shark has a unique pattern of spots and stripes.

The fastest shark in the ocean is the shortfin mako shark. It can swim up to seventy kilometres per hour!

shortfin mako shark

hammerhead shark

Hammerhead sharks often travel in large groups of up to one hundred sharks.

The largest shark in the world is the whale shark.

While most whale sharks are around twelve metres long, the longest one ever measured was nearly nineteen metres long! That's longer than a bowling lane.

The tiniest shark is the bioluminescent dwarf lantern shark. It is about as long as your pencil. So cute and tiny!

dwarf lantern shark

whale shark

leopard shark

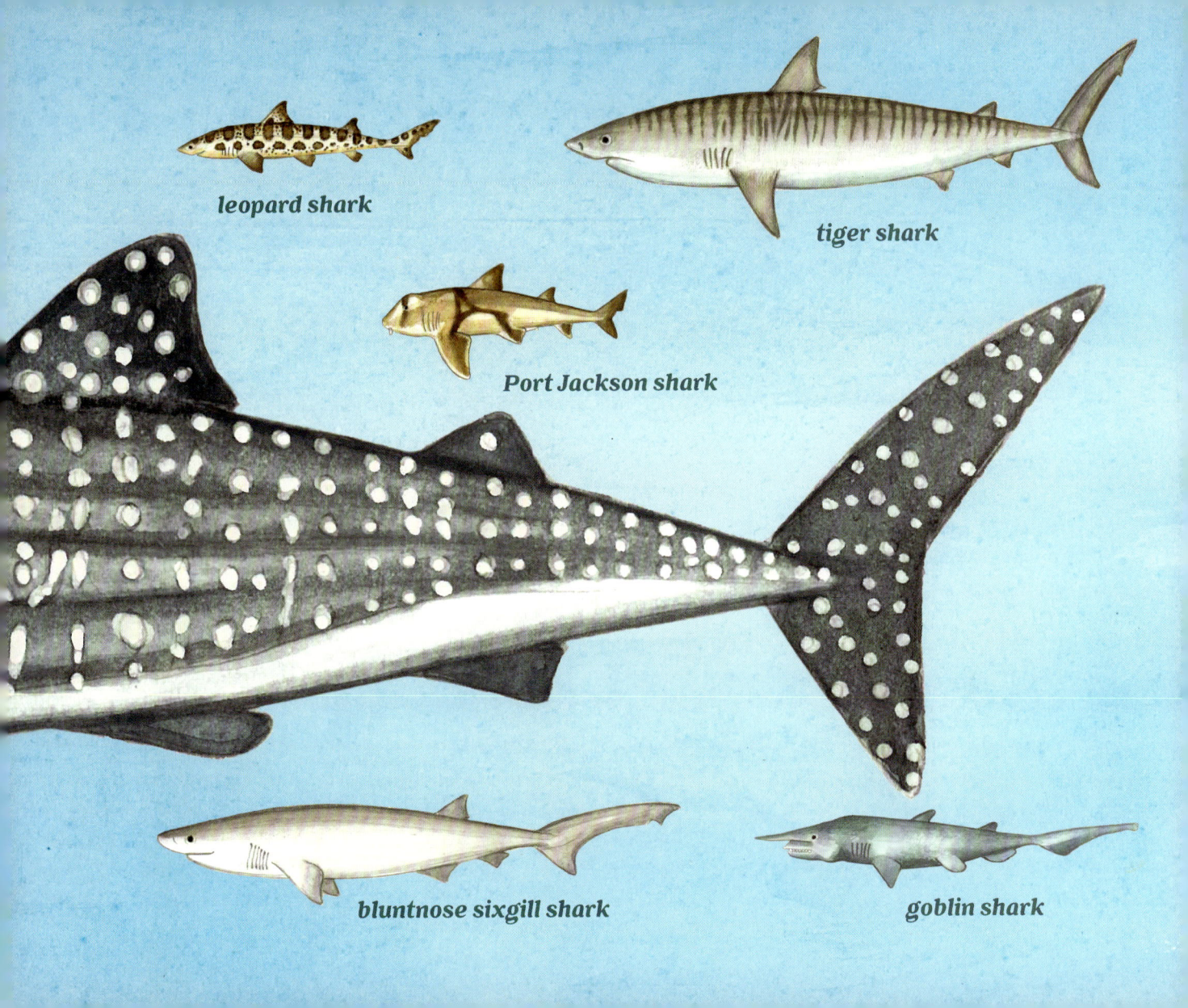

tiger shark

Port Jackson shark

bluntnose sixgill shark

goblin shark

moon jellyfish

Scientists once thought that no life existed below the 200-metre sunlight zone, but this next zone is, in fact, brimming with bright and flashy characters.

This is called the twilight zone.

firefly squid

viperfish

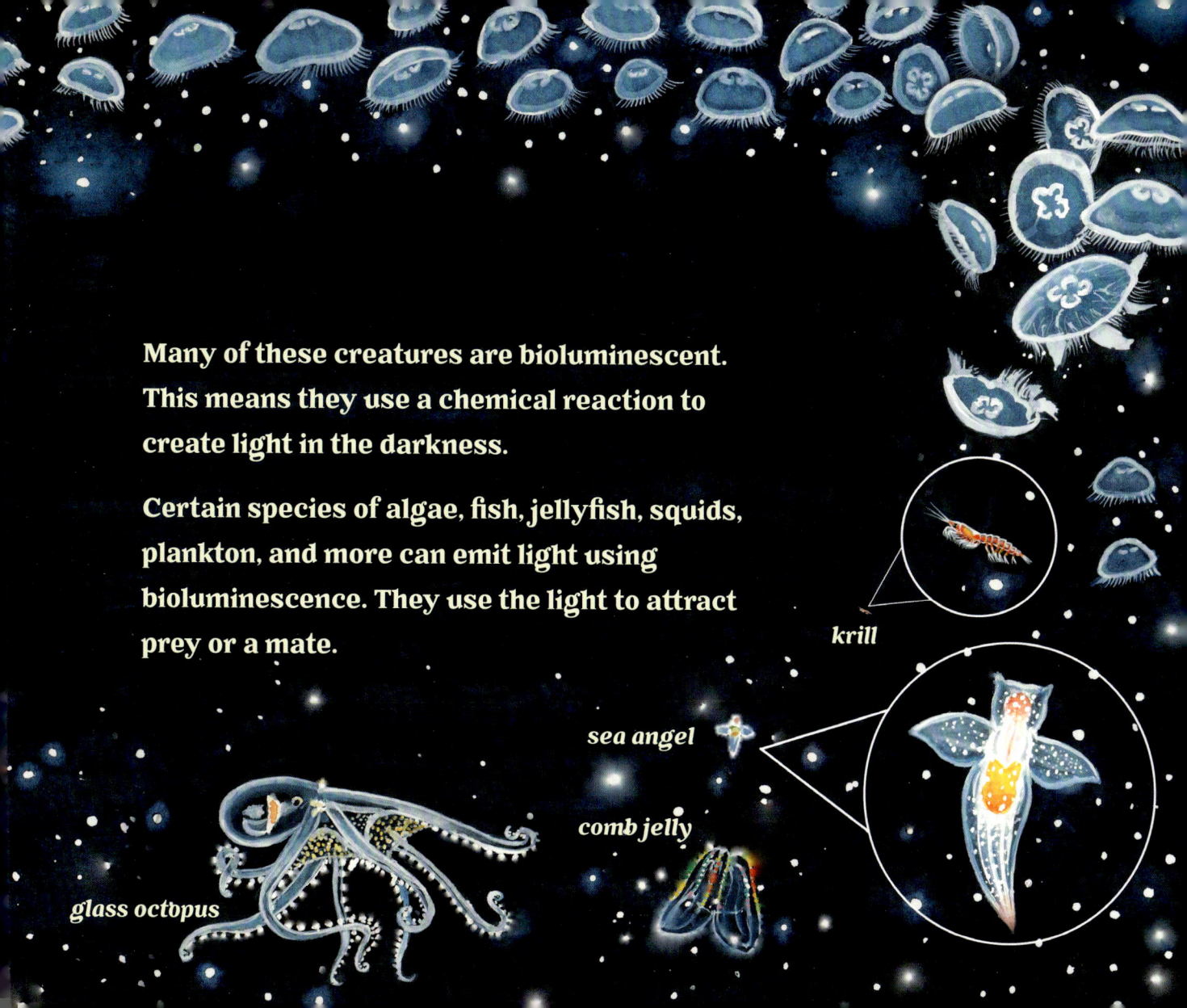

Many of these creatures are bioluminescent. This means they use a chemical reaction to create light in the darkness.

Certain species of algae, fish, jellyfish, squids, plankton, and more can emit light using bioluminescence. They use the light to attract prey or a mate.

krill

sea angel

comb jelly

glass octopus

One of the most intelligent creatures in the ocean often lives in the twilight zone: the octopus.

Octopuses have eight arms that they use to catch their prey. They also have three hearts and nine brains. (Yes, nine!) They are very crafty, can camouflage themselves, and have been known to escape their tanks in aquariums.

giant Pacific octopus

common cuttlefish

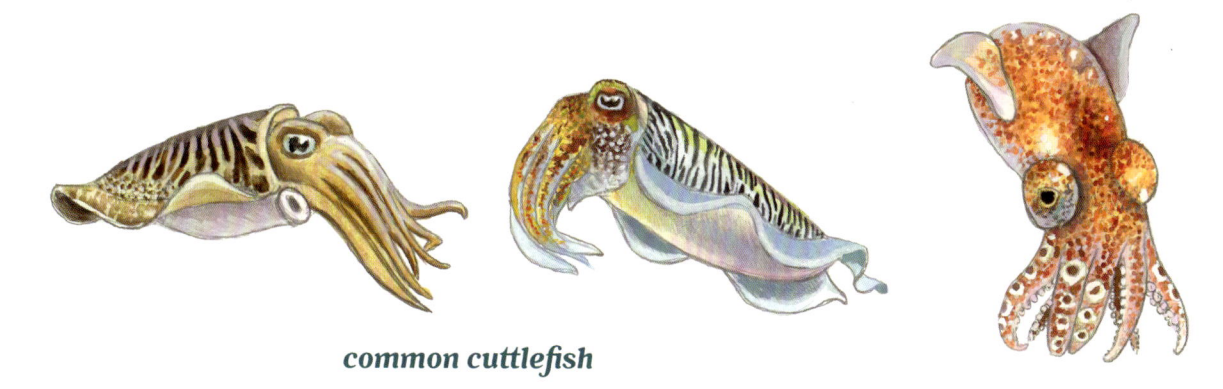

stubby squid

Octopuses are in the cephalopod family along with squids, cuttlefish, and nautiluses. Nautiluses, which are a type of ancient mollusc like a snail or clam, have been around since before the dinosaurs!

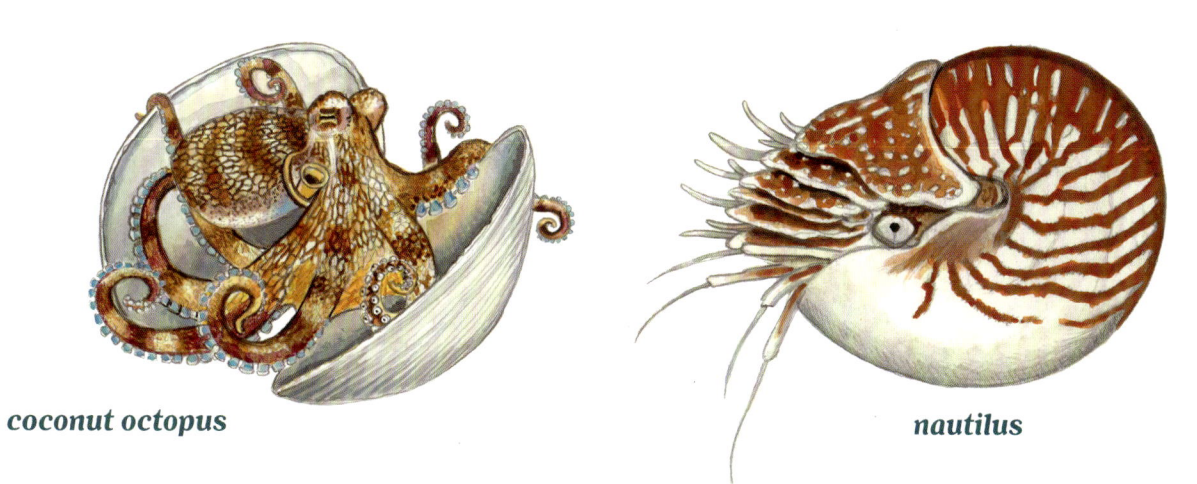

coconut octopus

nautilus

psychedelic jelly

leatherback sea turtle

Venturing deeper, we reach the midnight zone where no sunlight touches, but there is still so much life! Many creatures here are soft-bodied, like jellyfish and squid.

Other creatures come to visit the midnight zone, but don't stay long. The leatherback sea turtle dives down to hunt for its favourite food (jellyfish). Leatherback sea turtles are the largest sea turtles in the world and can grow to the size of a small car! Sperm whales also dive down to this zone to feed.

coral

Humboldt squid

sperm whale

There are even deep-sea corals that live in the midnight zone. They grow very slowly and can live for thousands of years.

phantom jellyfish

vampire squid

The deepest zone in the ocean is called the abyssal zone, and the deepest part of the abyssal zone is an underwater canyon found in the Pacific Ocean called the Mariana Trench.

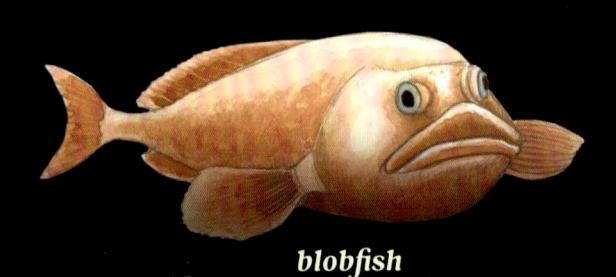

The abyssal zone is home to some pretty funny creatures. The blobfish doesn't have teeth and has a squishy body to handle the pressure of the depths in which it lives.

blobfish

The anglerfish has a little dangling light that attracts prey to its waiting jaws.

tube worms

Tube worms are one of the fastest-growing organisms on earth. They have gills that look like long red feathers.

anglerfish

The dumbo octopus has funny little fins that look like waving ears. They flap them to move along the ocean floor.

dumbo octopus

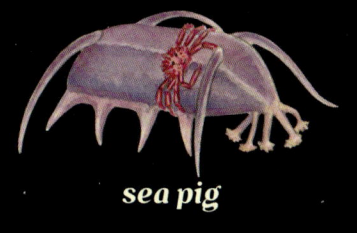

sea pig

The sea pig is a roaming deep-sea cucumber that allows baby crabs to ride on its back (or tummy) for protection.

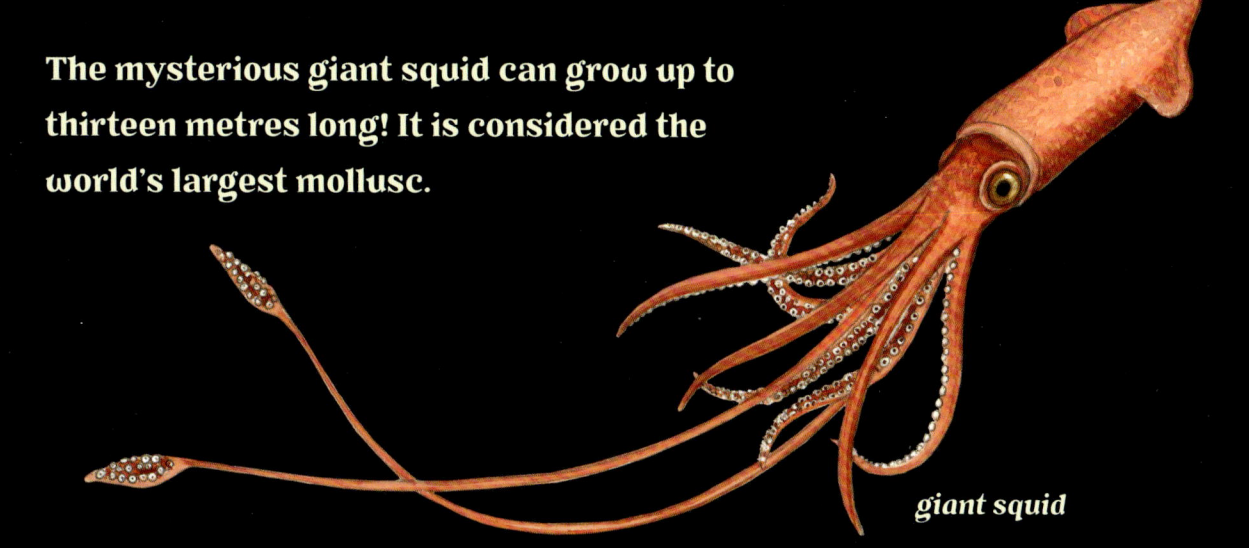

The mysterious giant squid can grow up to thirteen metres long! It is considered the world's largest mollusc.

giant squid

There is still so much to be learned about the world's oceans.

Next time you visit, what will you discover?